It's Laugh O'Clock

Joke Book

Valentine's Day Edition

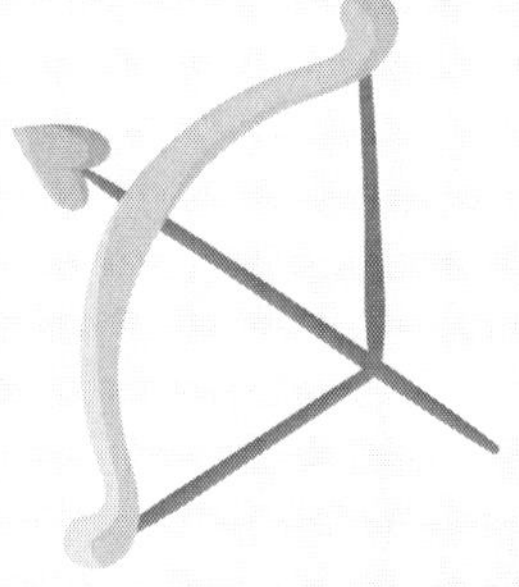

Hundreds of Jokes
That Kids and Family
Will Enjoy

RIDDLELAND

Design elements from Freepik.com

Table of Contents

Riddleland Bonus Book

http://pixelfy.me/riddlelandbonus

Thank you for buying this book. We would like to share a special bonus as a token of appreciation. It is a collection of 50 original jokes, riddles, and two super funny stories!

Join our **Facebook Group** at **Riddleland for Kids** to get daily jokes and riddles.

Introduction

"Life is filled with lots of things that make it all worthwhile, but none is better than your little smile."

Get ready to laugh! ***It's Laugh O'Clock Joke Book: Valentine's Day Edition*** is different from other joke books. This book is not meant to be read alone - although it can be; instead it is a game to be played with siblings, friends, family or between two people to see who can make the other laugh first. It's time to laugh; it's always laugh o'clock somewhere.

These jokes are written to provide a fun, quality reading experience. Children learn best when they are playing; reading is fun when it is something one wants to read, and most children want to read jokes. Reading jokes will increase vocabulary and comprehension. Jokes also have many other benefits:

- **Bonding** - Sharing this book is an excellent way for parents and children to spend some quality time having fun, sharing laughs, and making memories.

- **Building Confidence** - When parents ask one of the jokes, it creates a safe environment for children to burst out answers even if they are incorrect.
  This helps children to develop self-confidence and self-expression.

- **Improve Vocabulary** - Jokes are a lot of fun, and that makes reading a lot of fun. Children will need to understand the words if they want to understand the jokes.

- **Enhancing Reading Comprehension** - Many children can read at a young age but may not understand the context of words in the sentences. Jokes, especially puns, can help develop children's interest to comprehend the context.

- **Developing Creativity** - Funny, creative jokes can help children develop their sense of humor while getting their brains working. Many times a word in a joke can be taken two ways, and picturing it both ways leads to creative imagery.

- **Developing Logical Thinking Skills** - Because many jokes have a dual play on words, children must use logic to decide which meaning the speaker intended.

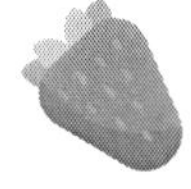

Enjoy the book, and, remember, it's always laugh o'clock somewhere.

Rules of the Game

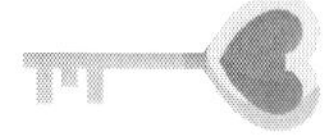

The goal is to make your opponent laugh

- Face your opponent
- Stare at them!
- Make funny faces and noises to throw your opponent off
- Take turns reading the jokes out loud to each other
- When someone laughs, the other person wins a point

First person to get 5 points, is crowned the Champion!

FUN FACTS FOR VALENTINE'S DAY

Did you know that Cupid and Eros are the same person?

In 700 B.C Greece, Eros was a God who could make humans fall in love by shooting his magical arrows at them. His name was changed to Cupid by the Romans in the 4th century BCE.

Do you know why an X represents a kiss?

It dates back from the Medieval period when people who didn't know how to write, would sign their name with a X. Then they kissed the X symbol, to show they were sincere.

CHAPTER 1

Valentine's Day Edition

"If you have only one smile in you, give it to the people you love." ~ **Maya Angelou**

What did one berry say to the other on Valentine's Day?

"I love you berry much!"

What did the cheese say to the cracker when they broke up?

I'm sorry. I'm just so much more mature than you are."

What did Robin Hood say to his girlfriend?

"Sherwood like to be your valentine."

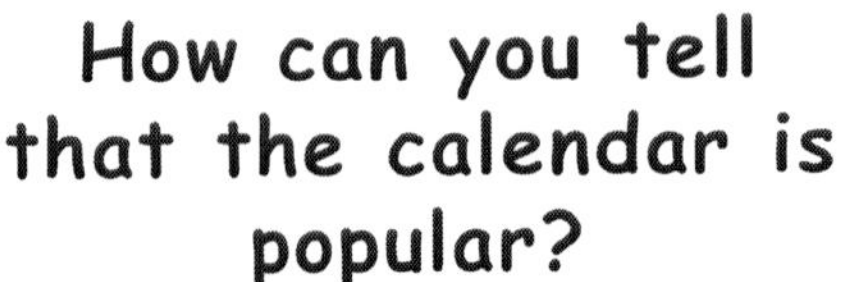

How can you tell that the calendar is popular?

It always has a date for Valentine's Day.

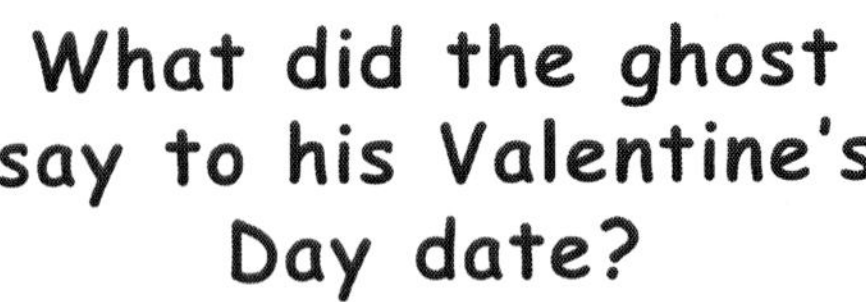

What did the ghost say to his Valentine's Day date?

"You look so BOOtiful tonight."

What did the calculator tell the pencil on Valentine's Day?

"You can count on me."

What did the cracker say to the marshmallow?

"I love you s'more and s'more every single day!"

What did the girl sweet say to the boy sweet?

"It's Valentine's Day and we're mint to be together."

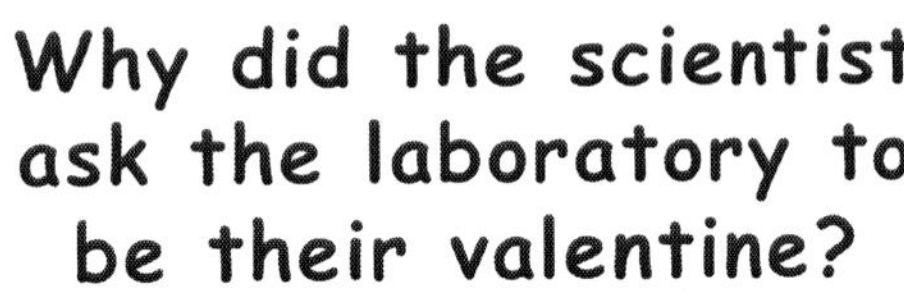

Why did the scientist ask the laboratory to be their valentine?

Because they had such great chemistry together!

What do you call a ghost's life partner?

His ghoul-friend.

What did the rabbit say to his wife?

"No bunny compares to you."

Why is Valentine's Day a good day for a party?

Because you can really party hearty!

What did the lightbulb say to his wife?

"I love you a whole watt!"

What is an astronaut's favorite chocolate?

A Mars bar.

Why did the apple go out with the prune?

Because it couldn't get a date.

What did the stuntman say to his girlfriend?

"Can I crash at your place and then watch television?"

What do you call two flowers that just started dating?

A budding romance!

What did the flower say to his valentine?

"I think you're dandy and I'm not lion!"

What did the flower's Valentine's Day card read?

Aloe you vera much!

If you are shopping for Valentine's Day gifts, the banker likes gold bars; do you know what kind of bars his wife likes?

Chocolate bars.

What do you say when you want a kiss from a flower?

"Plant one on me!"

Did you hear about the nearsighted porcupine?

He asked a pin cushion to be his valentine!

What did the baker say to his Valentine's Day sweetheart?

"I'm dough-nuts about you!"

What did the artist say to her sweetheart?

"I love you with all of my art."

Why did the policewoman lock up her boyfriend?

He stole her heart.

Where do burgers take their Valentine's Day dates to dance?

To the meatball.

What does toast call its valentine?

Its butter-half.

What did the flower say when it wanted a second date?

"I'll grow on you!"

What happens when you fall in love with a pastry chef?

You get buttered up.

What did the shy girl sweetcorn say to the boy sweetcorn on the evening before Valentine's Day?

"Shucks, I'd like to ear from you on Valentine's Day."

What did the boy apple say to the girl apple?

"I'm an apple and you're an apple, but I think we'd make a great pair."

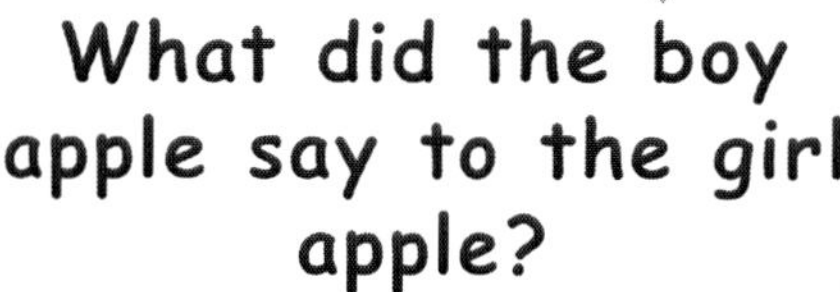

Why did the boy put clothes on his Valentine's Day cards?

He heard that they had to be addressed.

What did the hamburger say to its valentine?

"Time fries when I'm with you!"

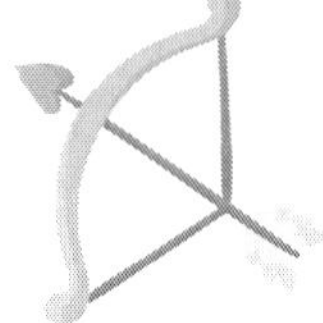

How did the mobile phone propose to his girlfriend?

He gave her a ring.

Why did the hotdog ask the bun to be its Valentine?

Because it really relished the time they had together!

Why was the taco so happy when the nachos asked it out for Valentine's Day?

It had bean hoping they'd ask all year!

What did the tree say to its valentine?

"I wood never leaf you!"

What did the cake say to woo its baker?

"You bake me crazy!"

What do you call a really small Valentine's Day card?

A valen-tiny.

Why did the boy call his girlfriend "Dictionary"?

She gave him meaning where there was none previously.

What did the blueberry say to his girlfriend on Valentine's Day?

"You blue me away and I love you berry, berry much."

What food is absolutely crazy about Valentine's Day chocolates?

A cocoa-nut.

What happens when prisoners fall in love?

They finish each other's sentences!

What fruits enjoy hugs the most?

Avo-cuddles!

How is love like wi-fi?

You must have a good connection for it to work.

What did the lemon say to the lime?

"Lime yours if you'll have me!"

Why did the romantic man call his girlfriend "Dentures"?

He couldn't smile without her.

Why should you marry a cherry?

They'll cherry-ish you forever!

Why do flowers drive so fast?

They put the petal to the metal!

Why did the calligraphist get lots of valentines?

Everyone thought she had pretty I's!

Why did the lunch box ask the banana to be its Valentine?

Because it really had appeal.

Why don't diabetic vampires like Valentine's Day?

They can't have sweethearts!

Why didn't the lady flower get upset when her Valentine forgot to buy her chocolates?

She rose above it!

What happened when the flower grew fed up with her Valentine's Day date?

She told him once and floral!

How does a flower handle a bad Valentine's Day date?

It gets clover it!

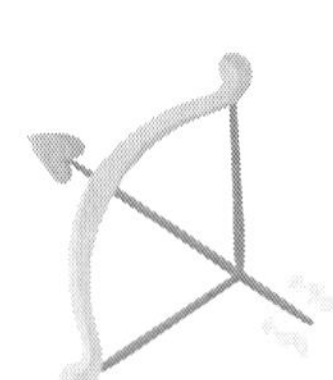

What flower gives the most kisses on Valentine's Day?

Tulips.

Why couldn't the teddy bear finish all its Valentine's Day chocolates?

Because it was just too stuffed.

Why do whiteboards get so many Valentine's Day dates?

Because they're so remarkable!

What's the difference between affection and adore?

You can't get your thumb caught in affection!

What did the pyramid say to its Valentine's Day date?

"Are you a triangle? Because you're acute angle!"

Why is it dangerous to give a Valentine's Day card to someone that is lactose intolerant?

They're all too cheesy!

Why did the doughnut visit the dentist?

She needed a chocolate filling.

Why did the lovestruck information technician get rid of his Google search engine?

Having found the love of his life, he believed there wasn't anything else worth searching for.

What happened to the travellers' relationship?

They grew distant!

What did the mermaid ask her valentine?

"Whale, shell we go dancing?"

What do ghosts say to one another to show that they care?

"I love BOO!"

What did the flower say to his wife when he brought her home a box of Valentine's Day chocolates?

"I hope thistle cheer you up!"

What do you have when your dad's two sisters' Valentine's Day chocolate candy melts in their hands?

Chocolate covered aunts.

What did the calculator say to its valentine?

"Let me count the ways that I love you!"

What did the coffee lover tell their Valentine's Day date?

"Words cannot espresso how much you mean to me!"

What did the tomato's Valentine's Day card read?

I love you from my head tomato!

How did Frankenstein ask his crush out for Valentine's Day?

"Would you be my Valenstein?"

How does Han spend Valentine's Day?

Solo!

What happened when two lazy people went on a Valentine's Day date?

They didn't work out!

Why do campers make for such great valentines?

They're always intense!

What did the paper clip say to the magnet?

"I find you very attractive."

Why does Miss Piggy have such good relationships?

She believes in Kermit-ment!

Why did the mushroom get a date for Valentine's Day?

Everyone thought he was a fungi (fun guy)!

Why does your heart want to be your valentine?

It's always pumped for you!

What did the pizza tell the delivery box?

"I love you with every pizza my heart!"

Why did the girl ask the air conditioner to be her valentine?

He was a big fan of hers!

What did the vegetable say to its valentine?

"You make my heart-beet faster."

Why didn't the blood cell have a date for Valentine's Day?

He tried to get one but his efforts were in vein!

How are a friendly, big, black dog and a chocolate factory which experiments with making Valentine's Day candy alike?

Both are chocolate labs.

What did one nacho say to the other nacho?

"This might be cheesy, but I think you're pretty grate!"

Why did the boy steal his valentine's glasses?

Because he heard love is blind!

What happened when the two tennis players met?

It was lob at first sight!

What's the cutest vegetable in the garden?

Cute-cumbers!

Did Adam and Eve ever have a date?

No, but they had an apple.

Why do skunks love Valentine's Day?

They are very scent-imental creatures.

Is it true that the woman who fell in love with the florist got happier and happier each passing day?

Well, her days certainly got rosier and rosier.

What did the honey dew say to the watermelon on Valentine's Day??

"You are one in a melon!"

What kind of Valentine's Day sweet is never on time?

ChocoLATE.

What's the best chocolate to get your girlfriend for Valentine's Day?

Her-She kisses!

Where do tightrope performers meet their Valentine's Day dates?

On-line dating sites!

What did the chocolate syrup say to the ice cream?

"I'm sweet on you!"

What happened when the two vampires went out for Valentine's Day?

It was love at first bite!

Why shouldn't you ask a tennis player to be your valentine?

Because love means nothing to them!

What did the Jedi say to her valentine?

"Yoda one for me!"

What did the romantic hydrogen atom say to the oxygen atom?

"I think we have chemistry together."

What did one mushroom say to the other mushroom on Valentine's Day?

"There's so mushroom in my heart for you!"

What did the drummer say to the other drummer on Valentine's Day?

"My heart beats for you."

What did the fruit cocktail tell its valentine?

"You're the pineapple of my eye!"

How did the vampire ask out his valentine?

He asked her out for

What does a carpet salesman give his wife on Valentine's Day?

Rugs and kisses.

Why should you never break a soccer goalie's heart?

Because they're a keeper!

What did the baker say to his Valentine's Day date?

"I only have pies for you!"

Why were the bears so madly in love?

Because they spent so much koala-ty time with each other!

What do you call two flowers that are best friends?

Buds!

What did the boy with the sprained ankle tell his Valentine's Day date?

"I've got a crutch on you!"

Why did the boy put the chocolate under his pillow?

Because he wanted to have sweet dreams.

What kind of flowers do you never give on Valentine's Day?

Cauliflower.

Why did the boy visit the doctor after Valentine's Day?

Because he heard that love was infectious!

Why did the barista ask out their valentine?

Because they were her cup of tea!

What is the most attractive kind of fruit?

Fine-apple!

Why did the boy give his Valentine tacos instead of chocolate?

He was thinking outside the box!

Why did the kid ask his maths teacher to be his valentine?

Because she helped fix all his problems!

What did the pastry say to its Valentine's Day date?

"I donut know what I would do without you!"

What did the flame say to all his friends when he found the perfect valentine?

"I found the perfect match!"

What did the ice-cream cone say when the sun asked it out for Valentine's Day?

"I'm so happy, you always make me melt!"

What did the pencil say to the paper?

"I dot my I's on you!"

Why didn't the skeleton want to send any Valentine's Day cards?

His heart wasn't in it.

FUN FACTS FOR VALENTINE'S DAY

Did you realize that one of the world's most famous buildings was a gift of love?

The Taj Mahal in India was built by Mughal Emperor Shahjahan as a memorial to his wife.

Do you know where is the most romantic place to live in the world?

Argentina. They don't just celebrate Valentine's Day for a day, they have a week to celebrate it. Also, there's another week set aside in July for 'sweetness week!'

CHAPTER 2

Sweet and Cute Animal Jokes

The Eskimos had fifty-two names for snow because it was important to them; there ought to be as many for love ~ **Margaret Atwood**

Why did the otter get married?

Because he met his significant otter!

What do you call two love birds on Valentine's Day?

Tweet hearts.

Why did the mouse ask the keyboard to be her valentine?

It was her type!

What happens if you kiss a dragon on Valentine's Day?

Third-degree burns on your lips.

What did the slug say to ask its crush to be its Valentine?

"Will you be my valen-slime?"

Did you hear the one about the bed bugs who fell in love?

They got married in the spring.

What did the owl tell its true love?

"Owl be yours forever!"

What do you call it when fish fall in love?

Guppy love.

How do you get a squirrel to be your valentine?

Act a little nuts!

What do you call the pigeon god of love?

Coo-pid.

Why do horses make great couples?

They have stable relationships!

What did the pig say to its Valentine's Day date?

"I won't go bacon your heart!"

What did the bat say to girlfriend on Valentine's Day?

"You're sure fun to hang around with."

What did the lizard say to woo his valentine?

"There are chameleon reasons why I love you!"

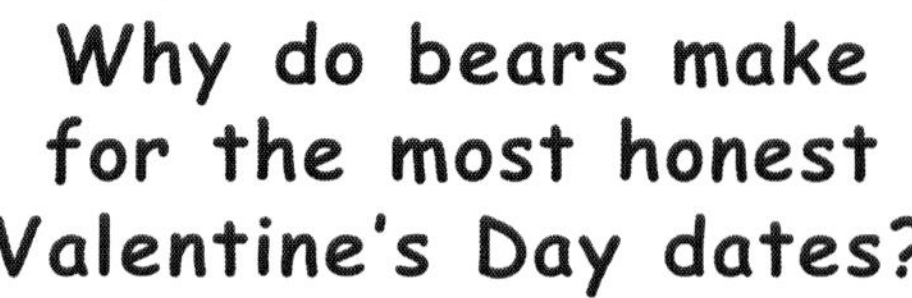

Why do bears make for the most honest Valentine's Day dates?

They can't help but bear their souls to each other!

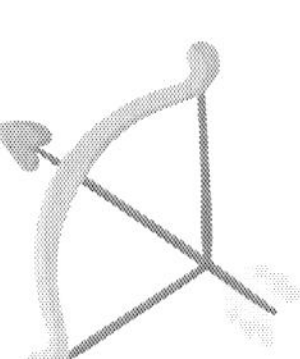

Why did the chicken cross the road?

Because her valentine was on the other side.

What did the deer say to woo his valentine?

"I'm very fawn of you!"

What did the tortoise say to his sweetheart?

"You're turtle-ly awesome!"

What did the tuna say to her boyfriend on Valentine's Day?

"I'm o-fish-ally in love with you!"

What did the whale say to his sweetheart on Valentine's Day?

"Whale you be mine?"

What did the bee's sweetheart say back to him?

"I love bee-ing with you, Honey!"

What do you call a sheep covered in chocolate and peanuts?

A snicker baa.

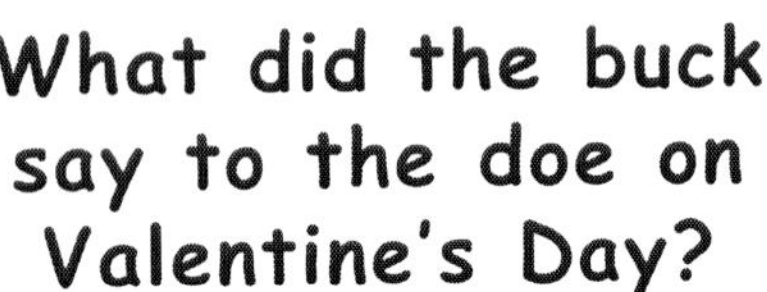

What did the buck say to the doe on Valentine's Day?

"You are very dear to me."

Is it true that the woman who fell in love with the florist got happier and happier each passing day?

Well, her days certainly got rosier and rosier.

What did the daddy sheep say to mama sheep on Valentine's Day?

"I love ewe!"

What did the girl sheep say back to the boy sheep?

"You're not so baaaaaaa-d yourself!"

What did the squirrel give to his valentine?

Forget-me-nuts.

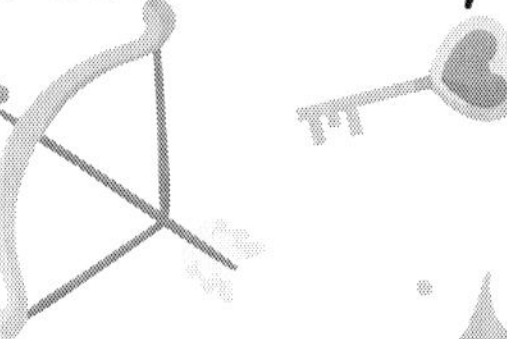

What did the snake say to her boyfriend on Valentine's Day?

"Come here and give me a little hiss."

How did the spider know she was in love?

Her boyfriend gave her butterflies!

What did the elephant say to her boyfriend on Valentine's Day?

"I love you a ton."

What did the dolphin say to its valentine?

"You give my life porpoise!"

What did the squirrel say to the his wife?

"I'm nuts about you!"

What did the wife squirrel say back to her husband?

"You're nuts so bad yourself!"

What did the rabbit tell his Valentine?

"Did you know some-bunny loves you?"

What do porcupines say when they kiss?

"Ouch!"

Why did the cats get married on Valentine's Day?

They were Purr-fect for each other.

What did the bee say to his Valentine's Day sweetheart?

"You are bee-utiful! Will you bee mine?"

Which one of Santa's reindeer can you always spot on Valentine's Day?

Cupid.

Why did the rooster cross the road?

He wanted to impress the chicks.

FUN FACTS FOR VALENTINE'S DAY

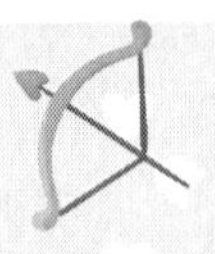

Do you know which invention was patented on Valentine's Day in 1876?

The telephone by Alexander Graham Bell. On Valentine's Day typically 11 million more text messages are sent on that day, compared to any other day in February.

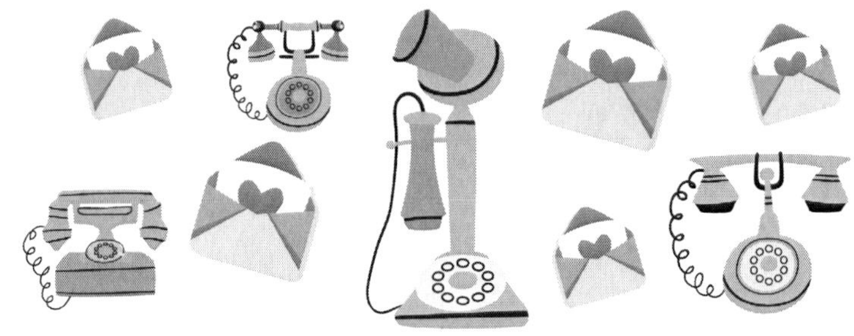

Do you know who Esther A. Howland is?

She's the person who first made commercial Valentine's Cards in America in the mid-1800s. Her cards included lace and ribbons. So, if you have ever sent or received a Valentine's Card in the US, this is partly due to her. It was profitable for her; she earned the equivalent of $3 million dollars each year.

CHAPTER 3

Q&A Challenge

"They invented hugs to let people know you love them without saying anything" ~ **Bil Keane**

What did the light bulb tell the light switch?

"You make my day brighter."

Why does Cupid keep his arrows sharp?

If he didn't, they'd be pointless.

Why did the old man call his valentine "dentures?"

Because he couldn't smile without her!

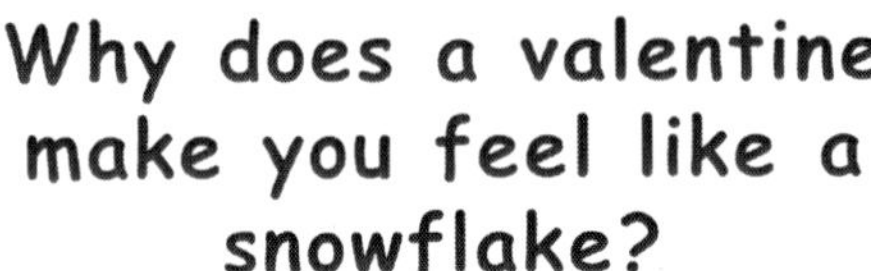

What did the astronaut's valentine say when he proposed to her in space?

I'm so excited, I can't breathe!

Why does a valentine make you feel like a snowflake?

Because you've fallen for them!

What's better than being madly in love?

Being happily in love!

Why does 1 love 0?

Because she's always around!

What's the perfect crime?

Stealing your Valentine's heart!

What do cavemen and cavewomen do on Valentine's Day?

Go clubbing!

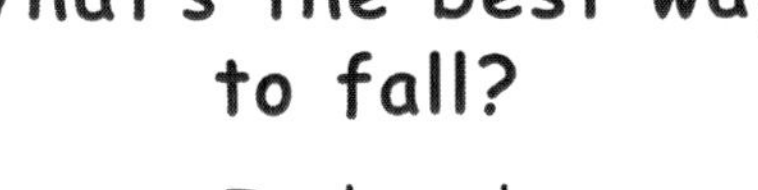

What's the best way to fall?

In love!

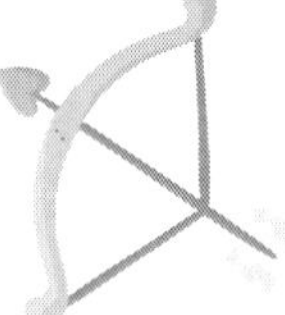

Who gets the most Valentine's Day cards every year?

The postman!

How do you know that a knife thrower really loves his partner?

He always misses her!

Why were the girl's feet getting cold?

Because her valentine knocked her socks off!

When isn't it romantic to steal someone's heart?

During surgery!

Why is your valentine like a camera?

Because you smile every time you look at them!

Why did the boy call his girlfriend his magnet?

Because he felt an attraction to her.

What do you call that feeling when you fall for your valentine?

Your common sense leaving.

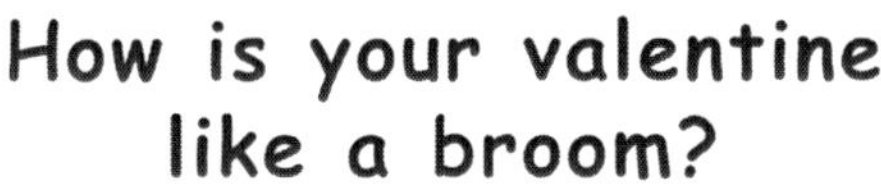

How is your valentine like a broom?

They can both sweep you off your feet!

Why isn't space a good place to take your Valentine's Day date?

It doesn't have any atmosphere.

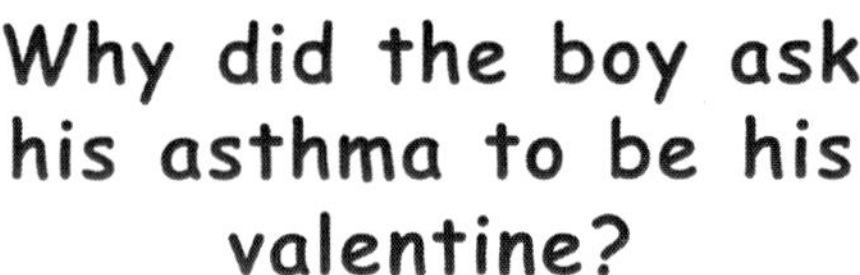

Why did the boy ask his asthma to be his valentine?

It took his breath away!

Why did the artist ask the colour green to be his valentine?

Because he loved it more than blue and yellow combined!

What happened to the couple who met in a revolving door?

They're still going around together!

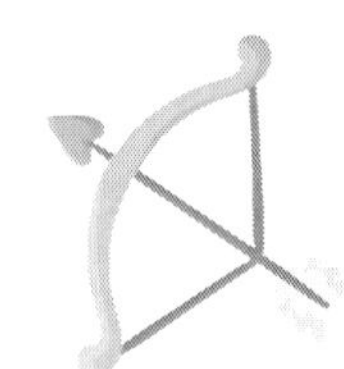

How do lightbulbs celebrate Valentine's Day?

They go out together!

What's the difference between like and love?

About two letters!

Are you a Pokemon?

Because I want to choose you!

How did the time traveler's relationship end?

It was over before it even began!

Why shouldn't you break somebody's heart?

They only have one!

What is it like dating gravity?

It has its ups and downs!

What indoor sport is Cupid the best at?

Darts.

What card game does Cupid always win at?

Hearts.

Why is a relationship without trust like a phone without service?

All you do is play games!

Why should you never make fun of your valentine's choices?

You're one of them!

What happened when the monster kissed his one true love?

He left his lip prints on the mirror!

What does a cupcake call their valentine?

Their love muffin.

What does Cupid always order with his pizza?

Wings.

Why are you and your valentine like a sock?

You make a great pair!

Why is lettuce the most loving of all the vegetables?

Because it's all heart!

What's the best part of Valentine's?

The day after when sweets are on sale!

Did you hear the one about the angels that got married on Valentine's Day?

They lived harpily ever after!

What do single people say to each other on Valentine's Day?

"Happy Independent Day!"

What vegetable makes the best valentine?

A sweet potato!

How do you show your valentine who's boss?

Hold up a mirror!

Have you seen a mailbox lately?

I have; I've seen girls box too.

What kind of bear has no teeth?

A Gummy Bear!

A doctor and a bus driver both love the same woman. Before going away on a long trip, the bus driver gave his sweetheart a bag of apples. Why?

Because an apple a day keeps the doctor away!

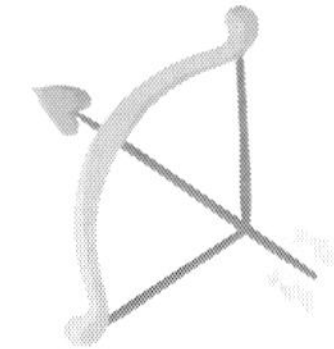

What did the envelope say to his stamp on Valentine's Day?

"I feel like I can go anywhere so long as we stick together."

What did the wax say to the romantic flame?

"You make me melt."

What did the hamburger buy his sweetheart on Valentine's Day?

An onion ring.

FUN FACTS FOR VALENTINE'S DAY

Do you know how many heart-shaped boxes of chocolates are sold each year?

36 million!!! They were started in 1860 by Richard Cadbury.

Do you know how many roses are produced for Valentine's Day?

200 million. Men buy almost 75% of these.

CHAPTER 4

Knock-Knock Jokes

"There's a long life ahead of you and it's going to be beautiful, as long as you keep loving and hugging each other" ~ **Yoko Ono**

KNOCK, KNOCK.

Who's there?

Pooch.

Pooch who?

Pooch your arms around me, baby!

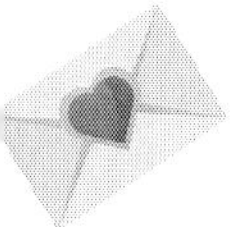

KNOCK, KNOCK.

Who's there?

Olive.

Olive who?

Olive you!

KNOCK, KNOCK.

Who's there?

Sherwood.

Sherwood who?

Sherwood like to be your valentine!

KNOCK, KNOCK.

Who's there?

Jamaica.

Jamaica who?

Jamaica valentine for me yet?

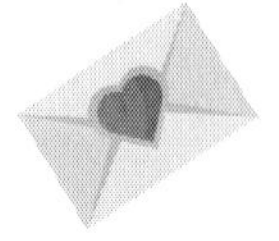

KNOCK, KNOCK.

Who's there?

Howard.

Howard who?

Howard you like a big kiss?

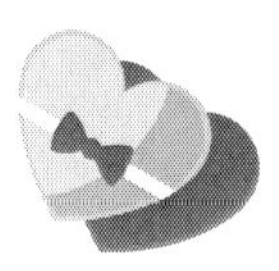

KNOCK, KNOCK.

Who's there?

Abby.

Abby who?

Abby Valentine's Day!

KNOCK, KNOCK.

Who's there?

Eyesore.

Eyesore who?

Eyesore do like you!

KNOCK, KNOCK.

Who's there?

Egg!

Egg who?

Egg-cited to be your valentine!

KNOCK, KNOCK.

Who's there?

Emma.

Emma who?

Emma hoping I get lots of cards this Valentine's Day!

KNOCK, KNOCK.

Who's there?

Fangs.

Fangs who?

Fangs for being my valentine!

KNOCK, KNOCK.

Who's there?

Fonda.

Fonda who?

Fonda you!

KNOCK, KNOCK.

Who's there?

Al.

Al who?

Al be your valentine if you'll be mine!

KNOCK, KNOCK.

Who's there?

Bea.

Bea who?

Bea my valentine?

KNOCK, KNOCK.

Who's there?

Honeydew.

Honeydew who?

Honeydew you want to be my valentine?

KNOCK, KNOCK.

Who's there?

Francie.

Francie who?

Francie being my valentine?

KNOCK, KNOCK.

Who's there?

Halibut.

Halibut who?

Halibut being my valentine?

KNOCK, KNOCK.

Who's there?

Iris.

Iris who?

Iris you were here!

KNOCK, KNOCK.

Who's there?

Iguana.

Iguana who?

Iguana hold your hand.

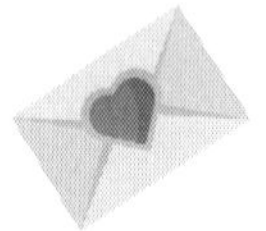

KNOCK, KNOCK.

Who's there?

Kisses.

Kisses who?

Kisses your lucky Valentine's Day!

KNOCK, KNOCK.

Who's there?

Zoo.

Zoo who?

Zoo you want to be my valentine?

KNOCK, KNOCK.

Who's there?

Iva.

Iva who?

Iva sore hand from knocking!

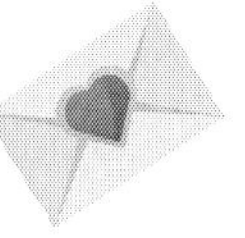

KNOCK, KNOCK.

Who's there?

Stopwatch.

Stopwatch who?

Stopwatch you are doing and have a happy Valentine's Day!

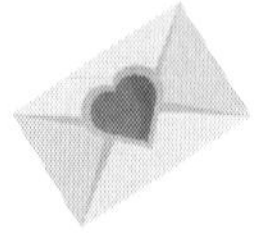

KNOCK, KNOCK.

Who's there?

Fiddle.

Fiddle who?

Fiddle make me happy if you would be my valentine!

KNOCK, KNOCK.

Who's there?

Dawn.

Dawn who?

Dawn go breaking my heart, Valentine!

KNOCK, KNOCK.

Who's there?

Aldo.

Aldo who?

Aldo anything for my valentine!

KNOCK, KNOCK.

Who's there?

Witches.

Witches who?

Witches the way to the Valentine's Day dance?

KNOCK, KNOCK.

Who's there?

Al.

Al who?

Al give you a kiss if you open this door!

KNOCK, KNOCK.

Who's there?

Amish.

Amish who?

Aw, how sweet. I miss you too!

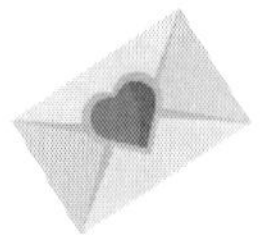

KNOCK, KNOCK.

Who's there?

Juno.

Juno who?

Juno I love you, right?

KNOCK, KNOCK.

Who's there?

Candice.

Candice who?

Candice be love I'm feeling now?

KNOCK, KNOCK.

Who's there?

Needle.

Needle who?

Needle a date for this Valentine's Day?

KNOCK, KNOCK.

Who's there?

Owl.

Owl who?

Owl be happy to be your valentine!

KNOCK, KNOCK.

Who's there?

Pauline.

Pauline who?

I think I'm Pauline in love with you!

KNOCK, KNOCK.

Who's there?

Mower.

Mower who?

I like you mower and mower every day!

KNOCK, KNOCK.

Who's there?

A door.

A door who?

I a door you!

KNOCK, KNOCK.

Who's there?

Cheese.

Cheese who?

Cheese a nice girl for being my valentine!

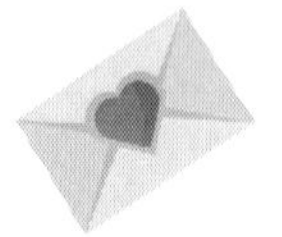

KNOCK, KNOCK.
Who's there?
Peas.
Peas who?
Peas be my valentine!

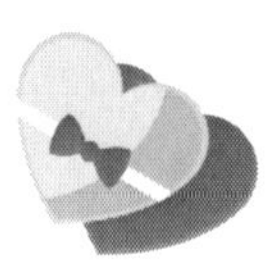

KNOCK, KNOCK.
Who's there?
Will.
Will who?
Will you be my valentine?

KNOCK, KNOCK.
Who's there?
Yule.
Yule who?
Yule never know how much I love you!

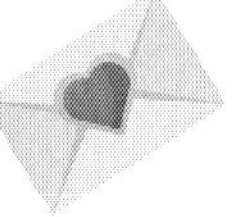

KNOCK, KNOCK.

Who's there?

Luke.

Luke who?

Luke who got a valentine!

KNOCK, KNOCK.

Who's there?

Mary.

Mary who?

Mary me, please!

KNOCK, KNOCK.

Who's there?

Orange.

Orange who?

Orange you glad that it's Valentine's Day already?

FUN FACTS FOR VALENTINE'S DAY

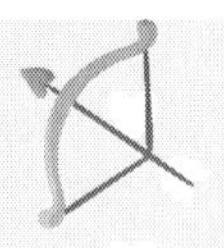

Do you know what is a great gift to give your Valentine who has a cough?

Conversation Hearts (or Love Hearts as they're called in the UK). Those chalky candy hearts that have messages printed on them, were originally designed by a Boston pharmacist, who changed from making cough drops, to creating candy in 1866.

Did you know that Japan kind of has two Valentine's Days?

The first is February 14th where women give chocolate to men; then on March 14th it is called White Day and men give women gifts of chocolates, clothing, and jewelry.

CHAPTER 5

Situations

"Love yourself first and everything else falls into line. You really have to love yourself to get anything done in this world." ~ **Lucille Ball**

A woman woke up on Valentine's Day morning and told her husband, "I had a dream that you gave me the most gorgeous and expensive diamond necklace I had ever seen as a Valentine's Day present.
What do you think it means?"
"You'll know tonight," her husband told her before he left for work. That night, the husband came back with a giftwrapped present for her.
Absolutely thrilled, the woman opened it up to find a book titled *The Meaning of Dreams*.

Two aerials met on a roof one Valentine's Day. They fell in love immediately and got married.
Their wedding ceremony wasn't very fancy but the reception was excellent.

A few days before Valentine's, a young student studied really hard to pass a maths test but the teacher was known for being a tough marker. When the student got his test back on Valentine's Day, he saw that he had a B-minus.
Hoping to change the teacher's mind, the student sent their maths teacher an expensive box of chocolates in the shape of a heart with an inscription that read "Be mine."
The following day, the teacher sent the student a late Valentine's Day card.
It read, "Thanks for the chocolates, but your grade is still be mine-us."

Matt wanted to get his girlfriend an expensive bracelet for Valentine's Day as a surprise so he went to the finest jewelry store in his city. After picking out a beautiful piece, the jeweler asked if he wanted to get his girlfriend's name engraved on it. After thinking about it for a minute, Matt decided to get it engraved to "His one and only."
"That's very romantic," the jewelery told him.
"Not really," Matt said, "This way if we break up, I can use it again."

On Valentine's Day, a young boy was walking through the forest that was filled with mushrooms when suddenly a talking fox came up to him. "Be careful where you step," the fox told him, "if you step on an orange mushroom then you will end up with the valentine of the ugliest person in the whole wide world."

The boy carefully watched his step, avoiding any and all of the orange mushrooms.

Suddenly, a beautiful girl appeared and approached him.

"I guess you're my valentine now," she told him.

"Why?" the boy asked.

"I just stepped on one of those awful orange mushrooms," she replied.

A beautiful girl spent all of Valentine's Day waiting to see what her boyfriend was going to get her. After school, she went over to his house for dinner. Instead of roses and chocolates, he surprised her with a plate of cannoli.

"What is this for?" she asked him.

"I cannoli be happy when I'm with you," he said with a wink.

Noticing that it was Valentine's Day next week, a boyfriend decided to see what his girlfriend desired. "What type of gift do you want this Valentine's Day?" he asked her.

"Well, I don't know," she replied coyly.

"Okay then," her boyfriend said. "I'll give you another year to think about it."

Becky and Sarah were drawing pictures in the living room of Becky's house. Sarah drew a picture of a knight rescuing a princess from a dragon and Becky drew a picture of herself and her neighbour, Ryan.

"Who's that?" Sarah asked.

"The boy next door," Becky answered. "Someday I'm going to marry him, you know."

"Why? Is he cute?" Sarah asked.

"No," Becky sighed. "But mum won't let me cross the street."

A couple was out to dinner for Valentine's Day when suddenly the girl looked over at her boyfriend and asked him, "Do you love me?"
"Of course I love you," he replied while looking at the restaurant's menu.
"Then whisper something soft and sweet in my ear," the girl told him.
Without taking his eyes off the menu, the boy leaned in close to the girl's ear and gently whispered, "Lemon meringue pie."

A plate decided to take out a fork for an expensive Valentine's Day supper. When the waiter came to take their order he asked if the plate and fork wanted it on one bill or two. **The plate looked at the fork and replied, "Don't worry, love, dinner's on me."**

A young boy asked his crush if she would be his Valentine. She told him she would but then the entire time that they were together on the playground, the young boy pretended that he was a Transformer. This annoyed his valentine like crazy. "If you don't stop that," she told him as she turned her back and walked away, "then I'm leaving.

"Wait," the young boy said with an outstretched arm, "I can change!"

A scary boy monster called up his girl-monster on Valentine's day to ask if she had received the big red heart he had sent her. "Yes, I did. You're so thoughtful," she said. "Thank you."

"Well," the boy monster said, "is it still beating?"

Sally was five years old. She loved sweets even more than her mother did. On Valentine's Day, Sally's father brought home a big box of heart-shaped chocolates for Sally's mum. The next day, the box of chocolates still had a lot of them left. Sally opened the box, reached in and touched one of the sweets. "Now, now, Sally," her mother said, "you will have to eat it now that you touched it." **Thinking for a minute, Sally reached into the box and swept her hand over the top of all the chocolates. "Well, now I guess I have to eat them all," she said with a smile.**

David wanted to ask Jessica to be his Valentine but he was too shy to just come right out and ask her directly. Instead, David approached Jessica at the end of class and asked her if she liked him. "Well," she said, "as far as boys go, I guess that you're alright." Smiling from ear to ear, David was about to ask her if she would go to the Valentine's Day dance with him when she continued. **"But the further you go, the better!"**

A handsome young Prince decided that it was time for him to be married. However, he couldn't just wed any Princess. The Prince would only get married to the most beautiful Princess in all the lands. He heard rumors of a great beauty on the other side of the world and so he set off on a grand adventure to find her.

After battling dragons and trolls and overcoming all kinds of obstacles, the Prince, at last, made his way to the Princess's castle and asked the Guards to see the King. Dressed in the finest clothing he could afford, the Prince confidently strolled up to the King and told him, "I have come from the other side of the world, having heard rumours of your daughter's beauty. I have battled monsters and beasts, braved storms and seas, all so that I may ask for your daughter's hand in marriage."

The king scoffed, "Well, you'll have to take the rest of her too or there'll be no deal!"

FUN FACTS FOR VALENTINE'S DAY

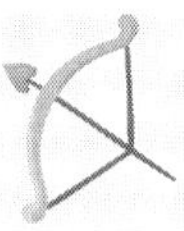

Did you know that in Finland, Valentine's Day is for everyone?

It is called Ystävänpäivä, and it is a day of friendship, where people give gifts of cards, flowers, chocolates, and teddy-bears, to everyone they care about. This includes friends, work colleagues, family, neighbors etc.

Do you know what Valentine's candy is still OK to eat a few years later?

Conversation Hearts have a shelf-life of five years!

Mine never last that long though!

Did you enjoy the book?

If you did, we are ecstatic. If not, please write your complaint to us, and we will ensure we fix it.

If you're feeling generous, there is something important that you can help me with – tell other people that you enjoyed the book.

Ask a grown-up to write about it on Amazon. When they do, more people will find out about the book. It also lets Amazon know that we are making kids around the world laugh. Even a few words and ratings would go a long way.

If you have any ideas or jokes that you think are super funny, please let us know. We would love to hear from you. Our email address is - **riddleland@riddlelandforkids.com**

Riddleland Bonus Book

http://pixelfy.me/riddlelandbonus

Thank you for buying this book. We would like to share a special bonus as a token of appreciation. It is a collection of 50 original jokes, riddles, and two super funny stories!

Join our **Facebook Group** at **Riddleland for Kids** to get daily jokes and riddles.

Would you like your jokes and riddles to be featured in our next book?

We are having a contest to see who are the smartest or funniest boys and girls in the world! :

1) Creative and Challenging Riddles

2) Tickle Your Funny Bone Contest

Parents, please email us your child's "Original" Riddle or Joke and **he or she could win a Riddleland book and be featured in our next book.**

Here are the rules:

1) It must be challenging for the riddles and funny for the jokes!
2) It must be 100% original and not something from the Internet! It is easy to find out!
3) You can submit both jokes and riddles as they are 2 separate contests.
4) No help from the parents unless they are as funny as you.
5) Winners will be announced via email or our Facebook group - Riddleland for kids
6) Please also mention what book you purchased.
7) Email us at Riddleland@riddlelandforkids.com

Other Fun Books for Kids!

Riddles Series

It's Laugh O'Clock Series

It's Laugh O'Clock
Would You Rather Series

Would You Rather Series

Get them on Amazon

or our website at www.riddlelandforkids.com

Riddleland is a mom + dad run publishing company. We are passionate about creating fun and innovative books to help children develop their reading skills and fall in love with reading. If you have suggestions for us or want to work with us, shoot us an email at riddleland@riddlelandforkids.com

Our family's favorite quote:

"Creativity is an area in which younger people have a tremendous advantage since they have an endearing habit of always questioning past wisdom and authority."
~ Bill Hewlett

Made in United States
North Haven, CT
06 February 2025

65506739R00052